LET'S DRAW! ANIMALS

Sr. Sanchez
Violet Peto

ARCTURUS

This edition published in 2022 by Arcturus Publishing Limited
26/27 Bickels Yard, 151–153 Bermondsey Street,
London SE1 3HA

Author: Violet Peto
Illustrator: Sr. Sanchez
Designer: Linda Storey
Design Manager: Jessica Holliland
Managing Editor: Joe Harris

ISBN: 978-1-3988-2027-2
CH010210NT
Supplier 29, Date 0822, PI 00001007

Printed in China

LET'S DRAW ANIMALS!

GLITTERING GOLDFISH

Draw another friendly
goldfish swimming
around this fish bowl.

CUDDLY CAT

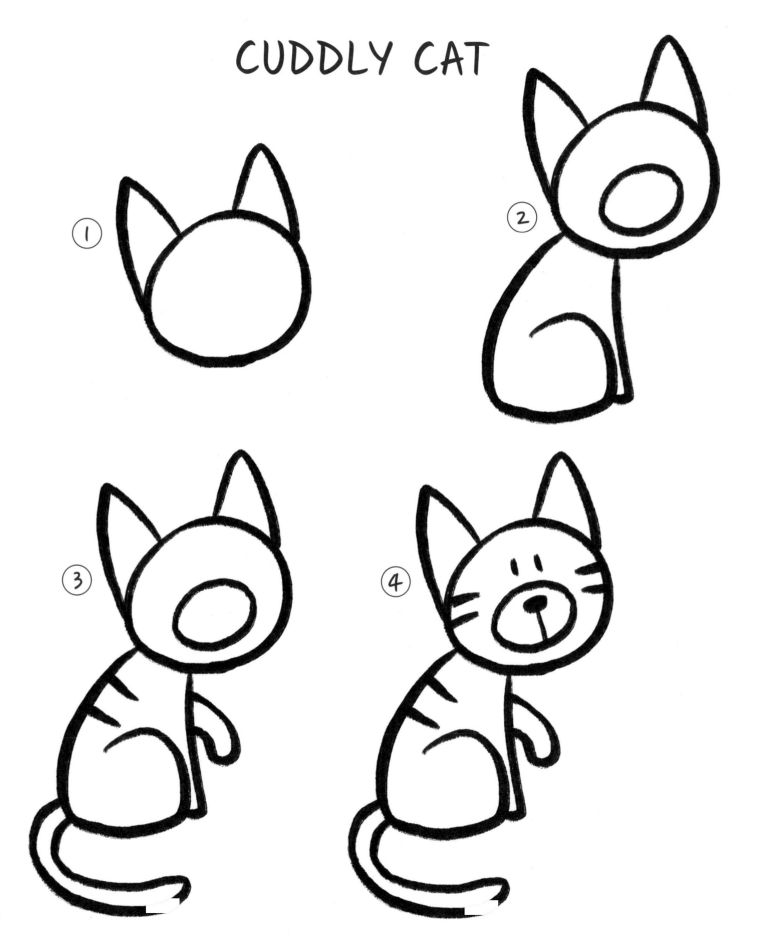

Give this cuddly cat a friend to play with.

GIVE THE DOG A BONE

Give this digging dog a pooch pal to help find the bone.

GREEDY GUINEA PIG

1

2

3

4

Add another hungry guinea
pig to the hutch.

LOVEABLE LOVEBIRDS

PRETTY POLLY

13

LIZARD LUNCHTIME!

Add another lizard catching locusts for lunch.

HAMSTER WORKOUT

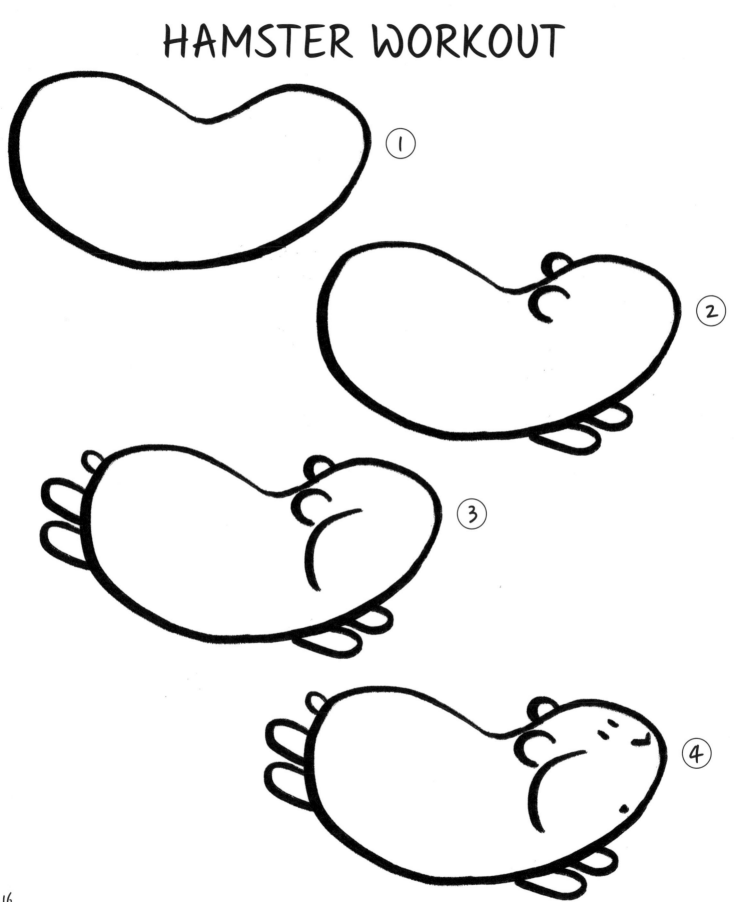

16

Give this hamster a gym buddy that's keeping fit on the running wheel.

SLEEPY BUNNY

Now draw some rabbits sleeping in their hutch.

WHEN THE CAT'S AWAY ...

Complete the troupe
of performing mice by
adding two more.

RUN FOR IT!

Sketch some more racing reptiles speeding along the track.

PLAYFUL PUPPY

Add some more playful pups making a mess!

FLUFFY KITTEN

Shhh, it's nap time!
Draw some more
kittens snoozing in
their basket.

WHAT A PIGSTY!

Add some more pigs wallowing in the mud.

MOO-VE OVER!

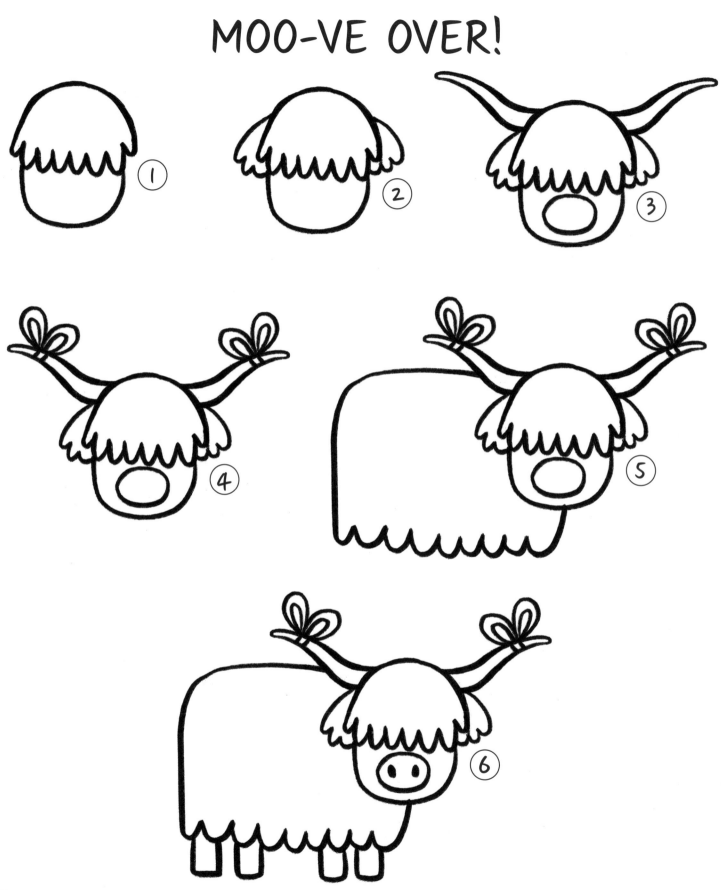

Give this cow some competitors in the cattle show. Who will take home the trophy?

COUNTING SHEEP

Counting jumping sheep helps you sleep! Add some more jumping sheep here.

BROODY HEN

RAUCOUS ROOSTER

NANNY GOAT

36

Goats will climb anything to reach food!
Put some more greedy goats in the tree.

HUNGRY HORSE

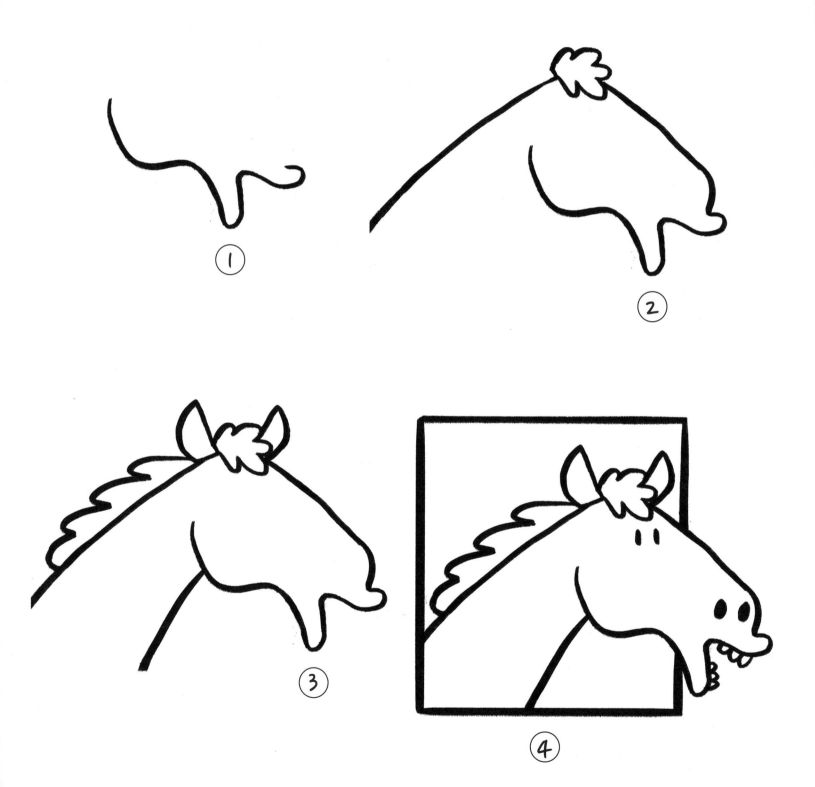

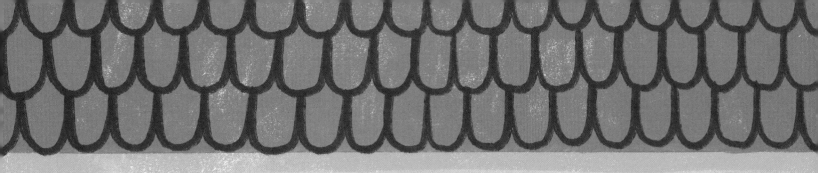

Fill the empty stalls with horses ready for their dinner.

IN A FLAP

This grumpy goose has surprised the duck. Draw some more flapping ducks to complete the flock.

DANCING DONKEY

Add some more donkeys jumping for joy.

GOBBLE GOBBLE

Give this turkey some friends to share grain with.

HERDING HOUND

46

Add more sheepdogs to help
herd these unruly sheep!

DIVING DUCK

Draw another duck diving into the pond.

49

TRUMPETY TRUMP

Give Nelly some friends to play with in the watering hole.

CROCODILE CONGA

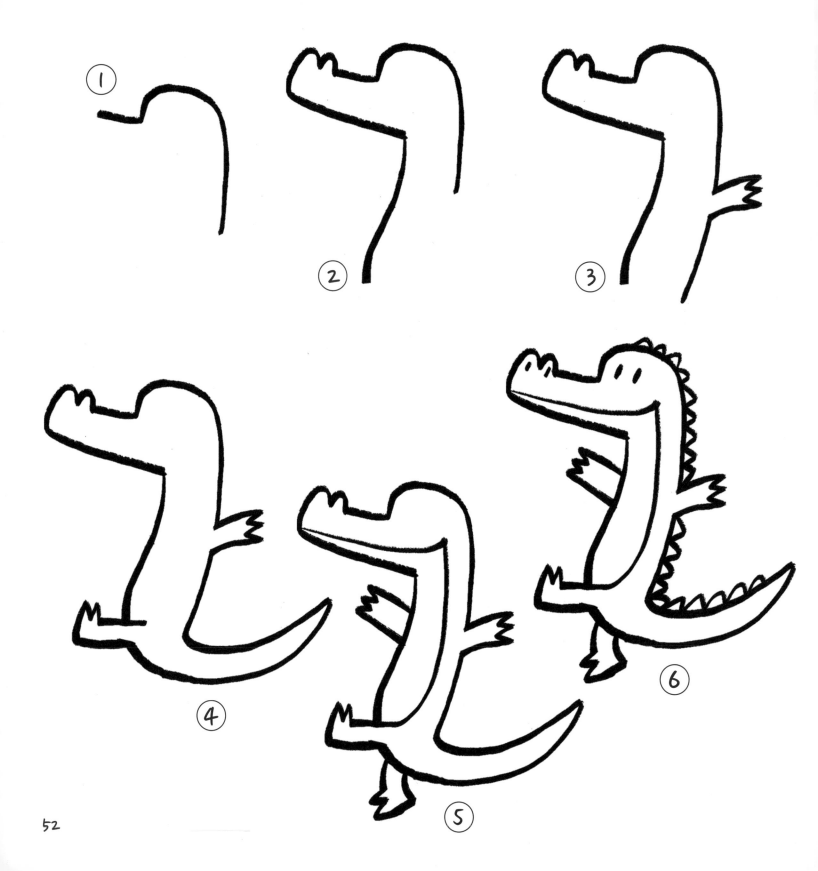

52

It's fiesta time down by the lagoon!
Add some more crocs to the conga.

FOREST FRIEND

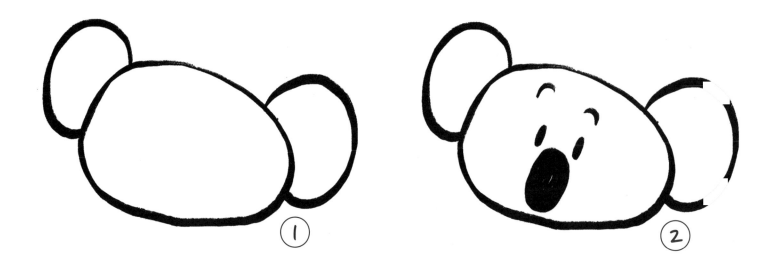

Draw some cute koalas climbing
the branches of this tree.

GANGLY GIRAFFE

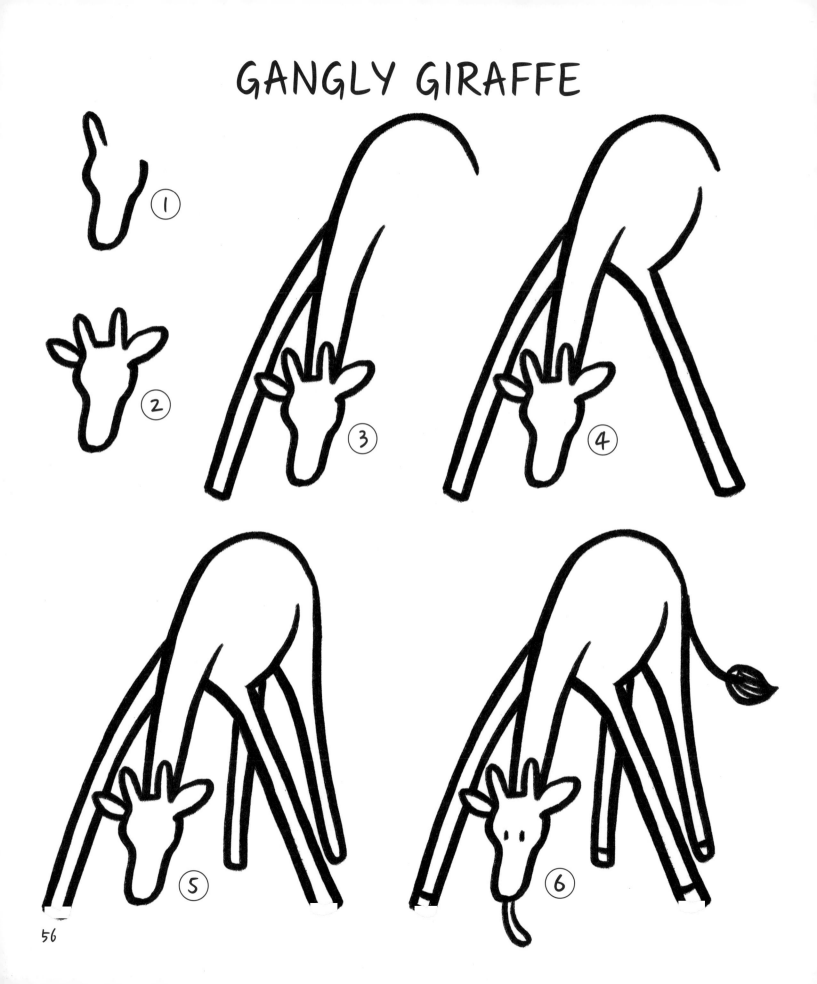

Draw another thirsty giraffe having a drink.

PEACEFUL PANDA

Draw another panda munching on bamboo.

HEFTY HIPPO

Add a few hippos to the herd.

MONKEY MAYHEM

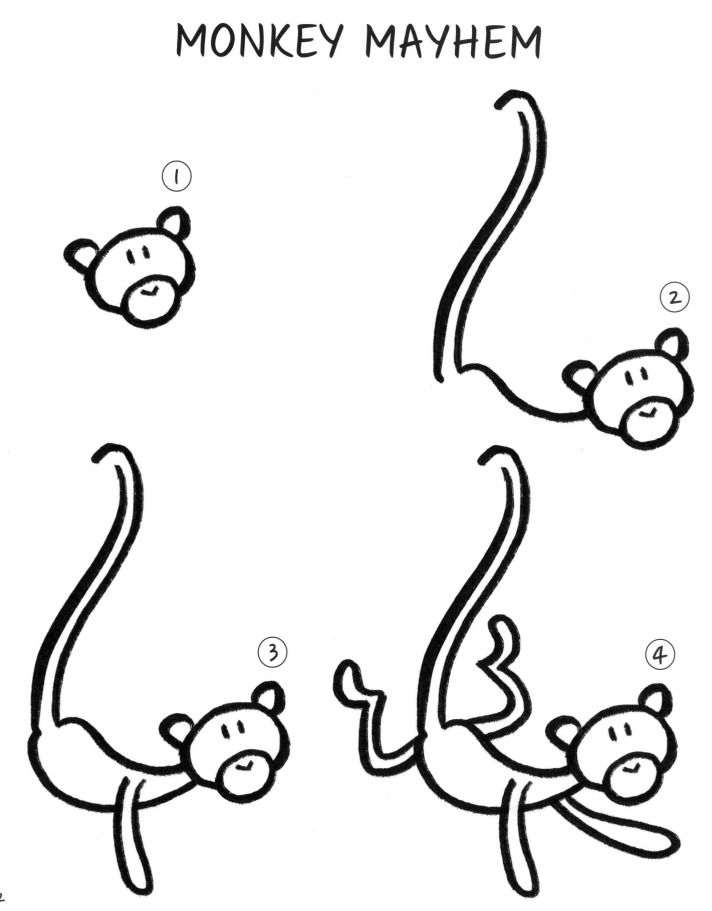

Draw several monkeys getting into the swing of it.

TOCO TOUCAN

We need two toucans! Draw the other parent guarding the nest of eggs.

BIG BROWN BEAR

Add another bear snuggled
in the cave for their winter sleep.

ROARSOME TIGER

Give this tiger some feline friends to help scare away the snake.

COOL CAMEL

Add another thirsty camel heading to the oasis.

71

SHARK ATTACK

WHALE TALE

CLOWNING AROUND

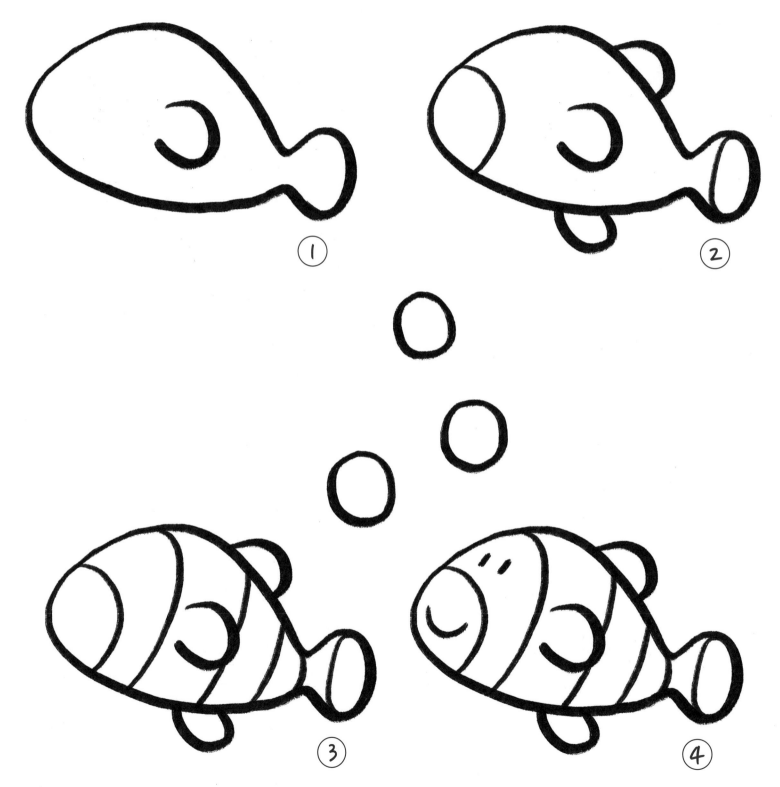

Draw another clown fish performing in the underwater circus.

LEAP FROG

Hop on down to the pond and add another friendly frog.

CUTE NEWT

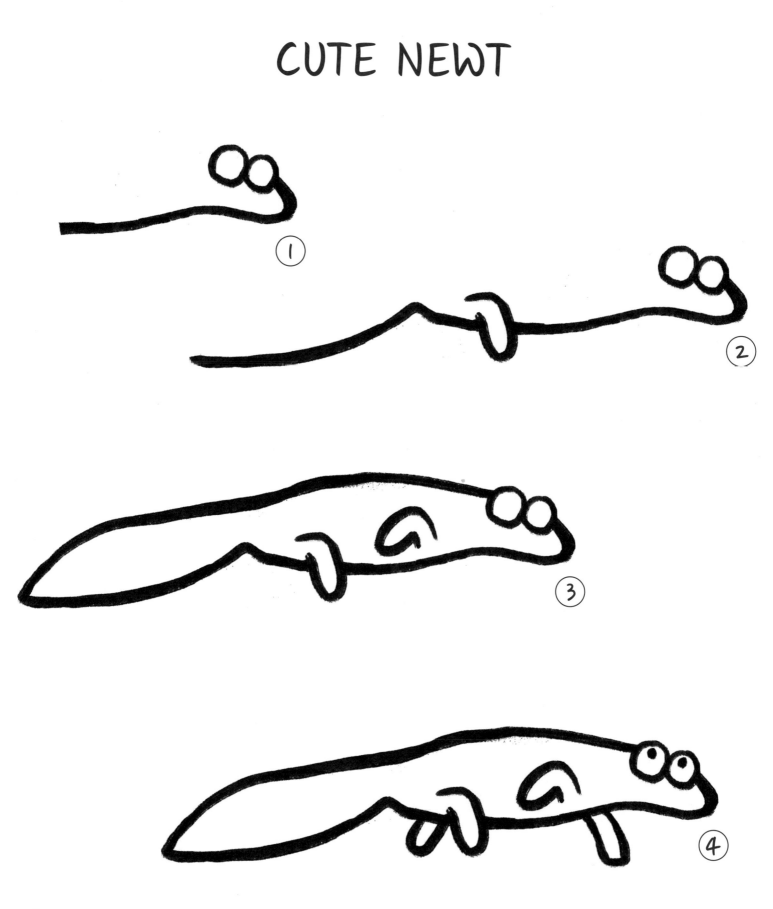

Draw a few newts hiding among the pondweed.

JOLLY JELLYFISH

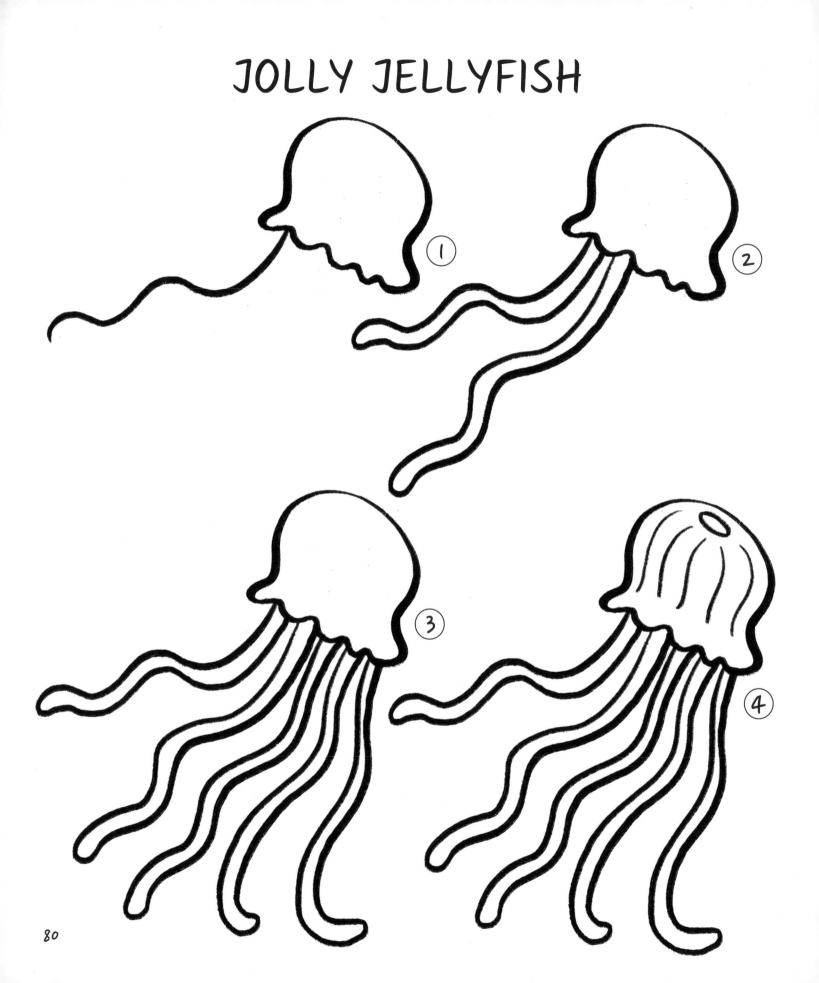

Add some more jellyfish
bobbing along in the water.

ALL PUFFED UP

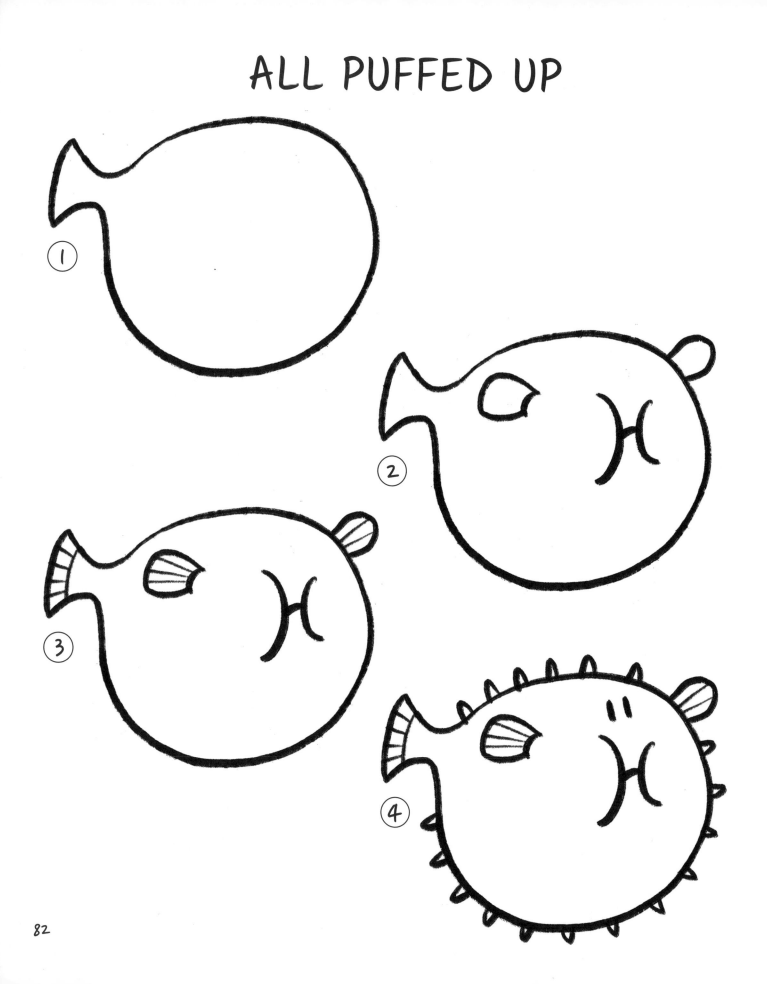

Fill this ocean scene with puffed-up puffer fish.

SLIDING PENGUIN

Add some more penguins slipping and sliding on the ice.

TURTLE POWER

Fill the beach with turtle hatchlings scurrying to the sea.

ADORABLE DOLPHIN

Give this dolphin a friend to play with.

PERCHING PELICAN

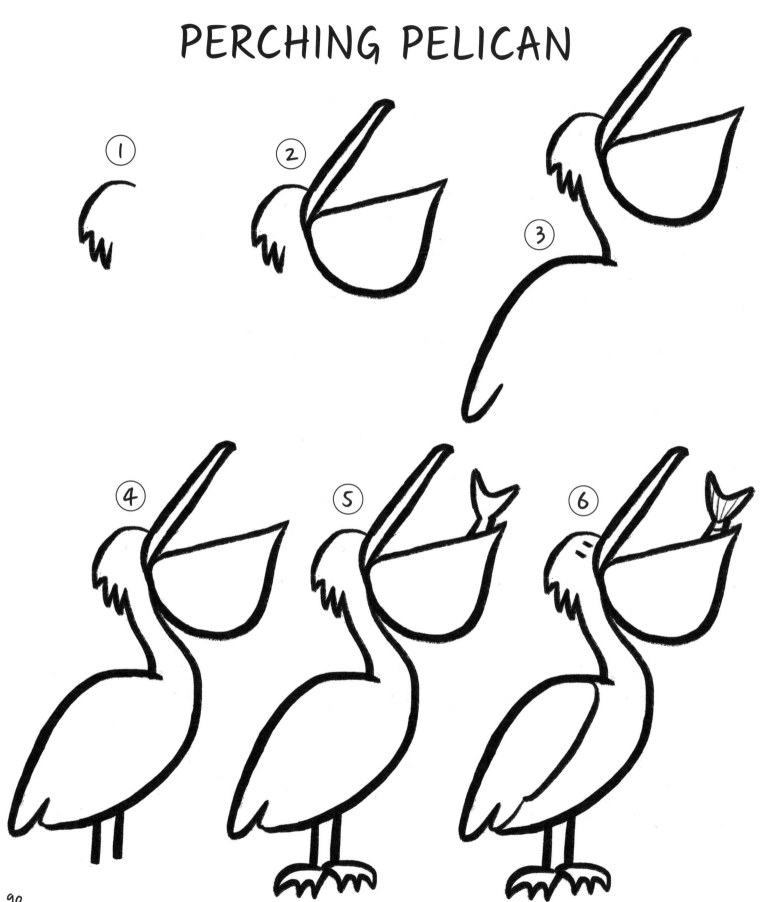

Add another
pelican roosting
on the rocks.

SLINKY SEA HORSE

Hide another sea horse in the pretty coral.

93

FLOUNCING FLAMINGO

Complete the flock
of flamingos showing
off their fabulous
feathers.

SUPER STARFISH

And do you know
who else is a star?
You, for completing
all the projects in
this book!